To John, thirty years later, better than ever
Love, T.R.

The editors would like to thank
BARBARA KIEFER, Ph.D.,
Charlotte S. Huck Professor of Children's Literature,
The Ohio State University, and
JIM BREHENY,
Director, Bronx Zoo,
for their assistance in the preparation of this book.

Visit us on the Web!
Seussville.com
randomhousekids.com

Educators and librarians, for a variety of teaching tools, visit us at RHTeachersLibrarians.com

Library of Congress Cataloging-in-Publication Data
Names: Rabe, Tish, author. | Ruiz, Aristides, illustrator. | Mathieu, Joe, illustrator.
Title: Who hatches the egg? : all about eggs / by Tish Rabe ;
illustrated by Aristides Ruiz and Joe Mathieu.
Other titles: Cat in the Hat's learning library.
Description: First edition. | New York : Random House, [2017] | Series: The Cat in the Hat's learning
library | Audience: Ages 5–8. | Includes bibliographical references and index.
Identifiers: LCCN 2016009989| ISBN 978-0-449-81498-7 (trade hardcover) |
ISBN 978-0-375-97171-6 (library binding)
Subjects: LCSH: Eggs—Juvenile literature.
Classification: LCC SF490.3 .R33 2017 | DDC 591.4/68—dc23

Printed in the United States of America   10 9 8 7 6 5 4 3 2 1

WHO Hatches the EGG?

by Tish Rabe

illustrated by Aristides Ruiz and Joe Mathieu

The Cat in the Hat's Learning Library®

Random House 🏠 New York

I'm the Cat in the Hat.
We must leave right away.
Can you guess what I'm cooking
for breakfast today?

Eggs! They're delicious
boiled, scrambled, or fried.
Come on and jump in,
and let's go for a ride!

Most eggs that we eat
come from chickens, it's true.
But eggs come from many
different animals, too!

Laying eggs is what birds,
insects, and spiders do.
Most amphibians, fish,
and reptiles do, too.

ALL LAY EGGS

insects

birds

spiders

MOST LAY EGGS

amphibians

fish

reptiles

When you look at eggs,
you find lots of surprises.
They have different shapes,
different colors and sizes.

This bird's egg is cone-shaped.
She laid it on this ledge.
Cone-shaped eggs cannot roll.
They won't fall off the edge.

MURRE EGG

10

n this egg are spirals
at help it to grip
n to rocks or in sand
the egg will not slip.

HORN SHARK EGG

Lacewings lay eggs on
stalks hanging from plants.
This helps to keep them
safe from hungry ants.

LACEWING EGGS

11

What shape are insect eggs?
Here we can see that
their eggs may be oval,
round, long, thin, or flat.

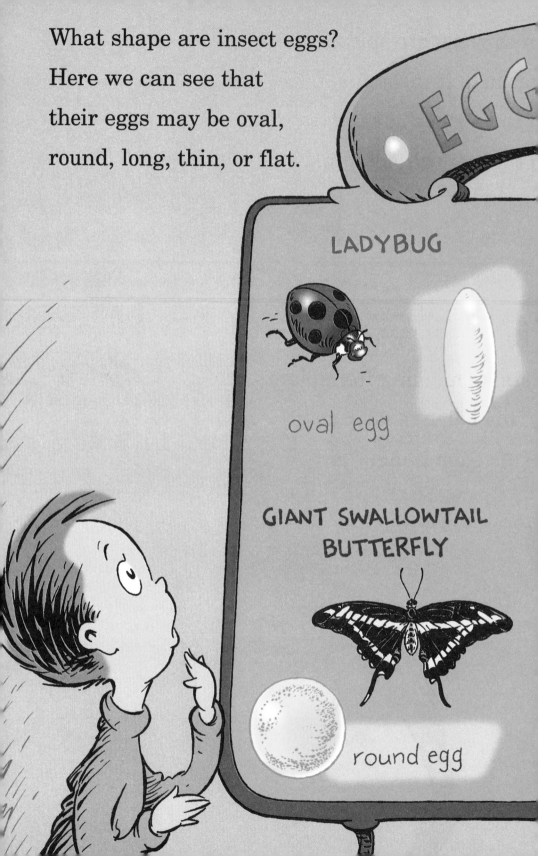

EGG

LADYBUG

oval egg

GIANT SWALLOWTAIL
BUTTERFLY

round egg

SHAPES

POLYPHEMUS MOTH

disk-like
egg

ANOPHELES MOSQUITO

long and thin egg

Eggs are all kinds of colors,
red, white, green, or blue.

SALMON
EGGS

TROUT
EGGS

GREEN-STRIPED
MAPLEWORM EGGS

CASSOWARY
EGG

EASTERN
BLUEBIRD
EGGS

EMU EGGS

TINAMOU EGG

CHICKEN
EGGS

APHID
EGGS

COLORS

Some have different patterns
like these eggs here do.

OSPREY
EGGS

PROTHONOTARY
WARBLER
EGGS

HONEY BUZZARD
EGG

GOLDEN EAGLE EGG

HARLEQUIN
BUG EGGS

GULL EGGS

CROW EGGS

OWL BUTTERFLY
EGGS

PATTERNS

Some mothers build nests
and lay their eggs inside them.
Nests are one way that
a mother can hide them.

CROCODILE EGG

A crocodile digs a hole
for her nest in the ground,

16

en covers it with dirt,
aves, and grass in a mound.

Not all nests are made
in the same size and shape.
This nest is a shallow hole
that's called a scrape.

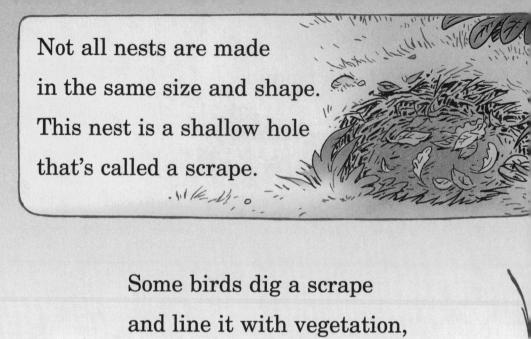

Some birds dig a scrape
and line it with vegetation,
which helps keep eggs warm.
It's natural insulation!

NORTHERN PINTAIL

A sea turtle crawls out
of the sea onto land,
and then digs a hole
for her nest in the sand.

Will she have boys or girls?
That depends on which part
of the nest they are laid in—
here, look at this chart.

Deep in the cool sand,
boys will likely be born.
Girls usually hatch
up where the sand is warm.

SEA TURTLE NEST

WARMER
SAND

WARMER
SAND

COOLER SAND

Not all birds build nests.
This owl, you can see,
may lay her eggs in
a hollow tree.

This cuckoo found a bird nest
and laid her egg there.
Then she flew off and left it
in the other bird's care!

CUCKOO

CUCKOO
EGG

WARBLER

Some mothers watch over
the eggs that they lay,
but some lay their eggs
and then leave right away.

A Nile crocodile
guards her nest day and night.
If a predator comes,
it is in for a fight!

NILE MONITOR LIZARD

This butterfly lays eggs,
then leaves them behind.
They are green and blend in
and are hard to find.

EASTERN
SWALLOWTAIL
BUTTERFLY

EGG

Some animal dads
are never about,
but some stay around
and are there to help out.

MIDWIFE TOAD

Till they hatch, this male toad
will carry his eggs
in long strings of jelly
that circle his legs.

To keep his eggs safe,
a dad jawfish will hide
the eggs in his mouth,
which he keeps open wide.

You can see for this dad
it is no easy feat.
For five to seven days,
he can't drink and can't eat.

A sea horse is a fish, and
what sea horse dads do
is give birth to their babies.
It's amazing but true!

This fish looks like a horse
with a long, curled-up tail.
The female lays her eggs
in a pouch on the male.

The male holds the eggs
in his pouch till the day
he gives birth to the babies,
which soon float away.

Most mammals don't lay eggs,
but monotremes (mah-noh-TREEMS) do.
A platypus lays eggs.
An echidna (ee-KID-nuh) does too.

PLATYPUS

ECHIDNA

An echidna lays an egg
that is oval in shape.
It is small and about
the same size as this grape.

ECHIDNA EGG

When it hatches, a baby
called a puggle breaks out
by using an egg tooth
on the end of its snout.

PUGGLE

A platypus digs two burrows—
a plain one for resting,
and one lined with leaves.
That one is for nesting.

She lays up to three eggs,
and as I have seen,
each egg is the size of
this pink jelly bean.

After three or four months,
her babies can swim.
They get to the water and
then glide right in!

How do little chicks grow?
I will show you the ways
a little chick grows
over twenty-one days.

The egg yolk provides food
while the chick grows in there,
and while it is growing,
it needs to get air.

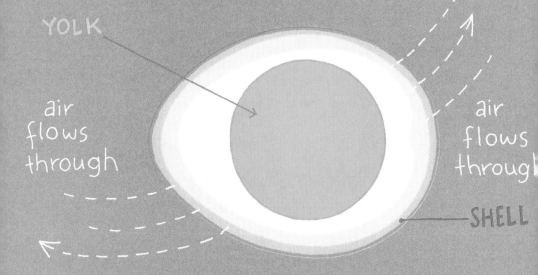

YOLK

air
flows
through

air
flows
through

SHELL

There are holes in the shell.
Through these pores the air flows,
in and out, out and in,
as the little chick grows.

This is the way
the chick looks on day three.
She's tiny and looks
like a small letter *c*.

EGG-U-BATOR

CHICK

YOLK

DAY-3

Here's the chick on day seven.
After only one week,
look closely—you'll see
she is growing a beak!

YOLK

beak

By day twelve, she can wiggle,
and bumps will begin
to pop out all over
the little chick's skin.

YOLK

These will turn into feathers.

It's day twenty-one.

The chick's ready to hatch.

All her growing is done!

EGG-U-BATOR

DAY-21

An egg tooth on her beak
helps the chick begin chipping.
The process of breaking the shell
is called pipping.

Cracking open the shell
is not easy and takes
all the little chick's strength
till the shell finally breaks!

ow she's out in the air.

er feathers dry quick.

ery soon she'll turn into . . .

a cute, fluffy chick!

In five or six months, she
will be fully grown
and able to start
laying eggs of her own.

GLOSSARY

Amphibian: A cold-blooded animal with a backbone tha[t] breathes using lungs and through its skin. Amphibians live part of their lives in water, and part on land.

Bantam: A small chicken.

Burrow: A hole in the ground that an animal digs for a home or hiding place.

Insulation: Material that holds heat or cold in or out.

Mammal: A warm-blooded animal that has a backbone and usually fur or hair and whose babies are fed with milk from their mother's breast.

Monotreme: A mammal that lays eggs.

Pipping: The process of breaking out of the shell of an egg.

Predator: An animal that kills other animals and eats them for food.

Puggle: A newborn echidna.

Reptile: A cold-blooded animal with a backbone that ha[s] scales, and lungs for breathing.

Snout: The nose, mouth, and upper jaw of certain animals.

Vegetation: Plants.

FOR FURTHER READING

An Egg Is Quiet by Dianna Hutts Aston, illustrated by Sylvia Long (Chronicle Books). An award-winning picture book about eggs, with beautiful, realistic illustrations. For ages 5–8.

Egg: Nature's Perfect Package by Steve Jenkins and Robin Page (HMH Books for Young Readers). Bold cut- and torn-paper collage images illustrate this collection of amazing facts about eggs. For ages 4–7.

The Emperor's Egg by Martin Jenkins, illustrated by Jane Chapman (Candlewick, *Read and Wonder*). An NSTA-CBC Outstanding Science Trade Book about the unique parenting arrangement of emperor penguins! For ages 4–8.

Where Do Chicks Come From? by Amy E. Sklansky, illustrated by Pam Paparone (HarperCollins, *Let's-Read-and-Find-Out Science®*, Stage 1). A simple introduction to the life cycle of a baby chick. For ages 4–8.

INDEX

amphibians, 9, 26
anopheles mosquitoes, 13
ants, 11
aphids, 14

birds, 9, 10, 14, 15, 18,
    22–23
butterflies, 12, 15, 25

cassowaries, 14
chickens, 8, 14, 34–41
chicks, 34–40
crocodiles, 16–17, 24
crows, 15
cuckoos, 23

eastern bluebirds, 14
eastern swallowtail
    butterflies, 25
echidnas, 30–31
egg teeth, 31, 38
eggs
    colors of, 10, 14, 25
    patterns of, 15
    shapes of, 10–13, 31
    shells of, 34, 38
    sizes of, 10, 31, 33

emus, 14

fathers, 26–29
feathers, 37, 39
fish, 9, 11, 14, 27, 28–29

giant swallowtail
    butterflies, 12
golden eagles, 15
green-striped
    mapleworms, 14
gulls, 15

harlequin bugs, 15
honey buzzards, 15
horn sharks, 11

insects, 9, 11, 12–13, 14,
    15, 25

jawfish, 27

lacewings, 11
ladybugs, 12

mammals, 30–33
midwife toads, 26